A Coastal Escape - Getaway for Families, Romance, Solos, Nature & History Enthusiasts & More

Northumberland
Travel Guide
2023

Curtis Kerr

Table of Contents

INTRODUCTION

Welcome to Northumberland

As you travel across Northumberland, you will enter a world of beautiful landscapes and deep history. This area, which is nestled amid the imposing coasts of northeastern England, welcomes you to discover its charming towns, magnificent castles, and amazing natural beauty. Northumberland has something for everyone, regardless of your interests—whether you're a history buff, a wildlife lover, or just looking for a peaceful getaway.

I found myself on the brink of a universe just waiting to be discovered as waves slammed against the rocky beach. Every adventure whispered in the sea wind beckoned me to go off on a quest of exploration. Northumberland got me under its spell with its wild beauty and alluring coastline.

I felt as if I could hear the echoes of years past as I gazed at the historic castles towering proudly on hilltops. The narrow lanes of charming towns appeared to be hiding mysteries from bygone eras, only waiting for inquisitive minds like mine to solve them.

I realized that this getaway was more than a holiday since it allowed me to get in touch with the spirit of a location as the sun sunk below the horizon and painted the sky with pink and gold colors.

A neighboring coastal café's aroma of fish and chips mixed with the salty tang of the air. Seagulls flying above and youngsters laughing while constructing sandcastles coexisted. This was Northumberland, a place of opposites where the past and present collided and where human life and nature coexisted in peaceful disarray.

I set off with a heart full of expectation, eager to get lost in the legends engraved into the landscape, to sample the scents of the sea, and to take pictures that would forever characterize my seaside getaway.

1.2 About This Guide

Your key to discovering Northumberland's riches is this guide. It is filled with insider advice, suggestions from the area, and necessary details to make the most of your trip and improve your travel experience. We've put up a thorough guide, covering everything from cultural exploration to beach experiences, to make sure your trip is smooth and enjoyable.

1.3 How to Use This Guide

It is simple to go via this manual. You may customize your investigation of Northumberland to your interests since each segment focuses on a different facet of your journey there.

You can get all the information you want right at your fingertips, whether you're looking for historical insights, practical planning advice, or the greatest locations to eat.

1.4 Getting Started with Your Travel Plans

Preparation is key, so spend some time doing it before you go on your Northumberland excursion. Information on discovering Northumberland provides the groundwork for a planned and memorable holiday, from picking the best time to go depending on the weather and local events to comprehending transit choices and creating an itinerary.

Get ready to be enchanted by the many landscapes, traditions, and cultures of Northumberland. As you explore the attractions of this seaside retreat, let this guide be your traveling companion.

2. Discovering Northumberland

2.1 Geography and Landscape

The topography of Northumberland is a canvas painted with a variety of sceneries, from broad coasts to undulating hills and verdant valleys. The western part is dominated by the Northumberland National Park, which offers untamed moorlands and historic woods to explore.

The Northumberland Coast Area of Outstanding Natural Beauty (AONB), to the east, has breathtaking seascapes, golden beaches, and towering cliffs. For hikers and wildlife lovers, the Cheviot Hills, which are part of the border with Scotland, is a paradise. You will see a wonderful fusion of ancient buildings and natural beauty as you go across the area.

2.2 Climate and Best Time to Visit

A maritime climate with pleasant summers and chilly winters prevails in Northumberland. It depends on your choice of when to go. The summer season (June to August) is well-known for its comfortable weather, which is great for outdoor activities and seeing seaside cities.

The cooler seasons of spring (March to May) and fall (September to November) are ideal for trekking and seeing historical sites without the summertime throng. With warm pubs, fun celebrations, and the potential to see the Northern Lights in the longer evenings, winter (December to February) reveals a new appeal.

2.3 History and Culture

The castles, Roman ruins, and medieval buildings of Northumberland bear witness to its turbulent past. Hadrian's Wall, which was formerly a Roman barrier, still survives as a reminder of that time. The castles in the area, such as Alnwick Castle and Bamburgh Castle, are evidence of the area's medieval heritage. Traditions abound in Northumbrian culture, and the county is home to a distinctive dialect that reflects its past and legacy. The ceramics and textiles produced locally provide a look at Northumberland's creative side.

2.4 Nature and Wildlife

The varied landscapes of Northumberland provide a home to a variety of species. Seabirds, such as puffins and terns, breed in the Farne Islands, which lie off the shore. On the rocks near the coast, gray seals may be seen relaxing.

Due to its designation as a Dark Sky Park, the Kielder Forest and Water Park is a refuge for observing birds and the night sky. The county's forests and open spaces are also home to red squirrels, otters, and deer.

3. Getting There and Getting Around

3.1 Transportation Options

Numerous modes of transportation are available in Northumberland to make it simple for you to get there and move about the area.

a. By vehicle: Renting a vehicle is a popular option if you value flexibility and the freedom to go to far-flung locations. The A1 and A69, two important thoroughfares, give access to Northumberland.

b. By train: The East Coast Main Line passes through the area and links Newcastle, Edinburgh, and London to Northumberland. Traveling by train provides beautiful views of the countryside.

c. By Bus: Towns and villages in Northumberland are connected by local and regional bus services. Buses are an inexpensive way to travel and discover places off the usual path.

d. By Air: Newcastle International Airport, which serves both local and foreign destinations, is the nearest major airport. You may drive or take a rail to Northumberland with ease from the airport.

3.2 Travel Tips

Research your alternatives for transportation and make a plan in advance, particularly if you want to use public transit.

a. Peak Seasons: To ensure that you get the lodgings and transportation that you want, make early reservations for both.

b. If you're driving, familiarize yourself with the local traffic laws. There may be twisting, narrow country roads.

c. Check the availability of parking before visiting well-known sites or town centers.

d. Train reservations: If you're riding the train, you may want to think about making reservations in advance, particularly for longer trips.

3.3 Northumberland Maps

Your exploring experience will be considerably improved if you have a map of Northumberland with you. Maps are readily accessible online, in bookshops, and in tourist information centers. Scales on maps vary from finely detailed town maps to more generalized regional maps. Some important ideas to remember are:

a. Pick up maps that emphasize coastal trails, walkways, and beach access sites for coastal excursions.

b. Historical places: You may explore Northumberland's rich past by using maps that highlight historical places and landmarks.

c. Countryside: Look for maps that emphasize hiking paths, bicycle routes, and nature preserves if you want to visit the countryside.

d. City Guides: Larger cities offer maps that emphasize nearby landmarks, lodging options, and services, such as Alnwick and Berwick-upon-Tweed.

With a map in hand, you can comfortably travel Northumberland's varied terrain and lovely towns, ensuring that you don't miss any hidden jewels.

4. Accommodation Options

4.1 Accommodations

To accommodate every traveler's interests and financial situation, Northumberland has a variety of lodging choices. You'll discover the ideal location to lay your head, whether you're looking for luxury, homey charm, or a rural getaway.

4.2 Hotel and Resort

The hotels and resorts in Northumberland provide convenience and comfort. There is a wide range of accommodations to choose from, including boutique hotels in old-world villages and contemporary beachside resorts.

The Bamburgh Castle Inn

This inn, which is conveniently located next to Bamburgh Castle, provides cozy accommodations with breathtaking views of the North Sea. It is popular among visitors due to its welcoming atmosphere, on-site restaurant, and close accessibility to attractions.

4.3 Bed & Breakfasts

By booking a delightful bed & breakfast, you can fully experience the welcoming atmosphere of Northumberland. These lodgings provide an individualized experience and often provide hearty breakfasts to start your day of travel.

The Old Post Office B&B

This B&B, which is situated in a charming hamlet, provides comfortable rooms decorated with antiques. It will seem like staying at a friend's house away from home thanks to the kind hosts who share local knowledge.

4.4 Cabins and Campgrounds

Northumberland's campsites and cottages provide a deeper connection to nature for those wanting a more rural experience.

Haggerston Castle Holiday Park, for example. This campground for families provides opulent hotels and campsites that are surrounded by lakes and forests. It's ideal for a fun-filled trip since it has entertainment facilities, indoor pools, and outdoor activities.

For Example: Cozy Coastal Cottage

A cottage rental near the shore provides seclusion and breath-taking vistas. While being just a short distance from sandy beaches and coastal paths, take pleasure in the comforts of a home away from home.

Regardless of your preferences, Northumberland's lodging options guarantee that you'll have a relaxing and enjoyable stay during your seaside getaway. Keep in mind to reserve early, particularly during busy times, to ensure your favorite option.

5. Exploring the Coastal Towns

5.1 Alnwick

Alnwick, a little market town located inland, is renowned for its historical importance and gorgeous architecture. Discover the historic Alnwick Castle, which has appeared in many movies and television series, including Harry Potter.

Explore the exquisitely designed Alnwick Garden, which has fountains, treehouses, and rare plant collections. A bibliophile's haven, The Barter Books is located in a historic railroad station. In the quaint café, find hidden local literary treasures and relax with a cup of tea.

Alnwick Castle and Gardens, Barter Books, and Bailiffgate Museum are must-sees.

5.2 Bamburgh

This seaside village has a classic charm thanks to Bamburgh Castle as a background. With its towering presence and breathtaking vistas of the North Sea, Bamburgh Castle commands the skyline. Bamburgh Beach is a large stretch of golden sand ideal for leisurely walks and picnics. Stroll along it.

Visit the Grace Darling Museum to learn about the bravery of the lighthouse keeper who assisted in the shipwreck rescue of survivors. Don't pass up the chance to see breathtaking sunsets against the outline of the castle.

Must-sees include Bamburgh Beach, the Grace Darling Museum, and Bamburgh Castle.

5.3 Seahouses

Seahouses, which is well-known as the entrance to the Farne Islands, is a thriving fishing community with a lot to offer. Visit the Farne

Islands, a haven for seabirds and seals, via boat from Seahouses Harbour. Wander around the port, where you may find modest shops and places to have fish & chips. Visit the RNLI Grace Darling Museum to learn about the heroic local's life. An excellent starting point for seeing neighboring sites including Beadnell Bay and the picturesque Northumberland Coast Path is Seahouses.

Farne Islands Boat Tours, the RNLI Grace Darling Museum, and Seahouses Harbour are must-sees.

5.4 Berwick-upon-Tweed

Berwick-upon-Tweed, which is located at the northernmost point of England, has a long history that has been molded by its advantageous position. Discover the town's Elizabethan Walls, which enclose it and provide sweeping views of the sea.

Visit the Berwick Barracks, a former military facility that is now home to a museum highlighting the history of the community. From plays to movie showings, The Maltings Theatre & Cinema provides a range of cultural activities. The town is an interesting visit for history aficionados due to its distinctive fusion of English and Scottish influences, which is seen in its architecture.

The Maltings Theatre & Cinema, Berwick Barracks, and the Berwick Walls are all must-sees.

5.5 Additional Coastal Towns
Northumberland's less well-known seaside communities provide peaceful retreats and genuine experiences away from the limelight.

a. Seaton Point is a serene community with a beautiful sandy beach that is ideal for relaxing and taking strolls.

b. Craster: A charming community with a lovely port that is well-known for its kippers. Visit the stunning coastal ruin of Dunstanburgh Castle.

c. Low Newton-by-the-Sea: This little village provides a tranquil setting. Views of Embleton Bay may be seen while drinking a beer at the Ship Inn.

d. Amble: This thriving fishing town, complete with a marina, is well-known for its seafood and vivacious local culture.

e. Seahouses is a bustling base for visiting the Farne Islands and is home to several tourist attractions.

Each community has its distinct beauty waiting to be found, from ancient monuments to peaceful beaches.

6. Coastal Activities

6.1 Beaches and Seaside Fun

The coastline of Northumberland provides a playground of sandy beaches and chances for leisurely seaside activities. At beaches like Bamburgh Beach, Embleton Bay, and Druridge Bay, spend the day making sandcastles, having a picnic, and taking in the sea air. Your four-legged pet may also enjoy the seaside since many beaches are dog-friendly. For a fun and instructive experience, don't forget to explore rock pools and look for shells during low tide.

5.2 Water Sports

Northumberland's waterways are ideal for lovers of water sports for those looking for more physically demanding activities. Surfing classes are available in Beadnell Bay for all ability levels, so give it a try.

The nooks and crannies of the coastline may be explored by kayaking, paddleboarding, and coasteering. You may take boat cruises from Seahouses and Amble to see the Farne Islands' fauna and historical monuments up close.

5.3 Walking and Hiking Trails

Northumberland is a hiker and walker's heaven due to its diverse scenery. The Northumberland Coast Path provides beautiful scenery and the opportunity to visit coastal communities along the route. For experienced hikers, the Cheviot Hills provide difficult terrain, while shorter paths like the St. Cuthbert's Way offer more relaxing choices. Be on the lookout for a variety of species, including red squirrels and seagulls.

5.4 Cycling Routes

Cycling is a great way to take your time and enjoy Northumberland's beauty. Along with passing through quaint communities and historic attractions, the Coast and Castles Cycle Route follows the shoreline. A mountain bike route that highlights the county's varied topography is called The Sandstone Way. The Wannie Line provides a path along an abandoned railroad that is suitable for families.

The coastal activities in Northumberland are suitable for people of all ages and interests, ranging from leisurely beach time to exhilarating water sports. The seaside area delivers a variety of unforgettable experiences, whether you're an adrenaline addict or a nature enthusiast.

6. Cultural and Historical Sites

6.1 Forts and Castles

A patchwork of castles and forts, each with its distinct narrative to tell, punctuate Northumberland's history.

a. Alnwick Castle is a magnificent medieval structure well-known for serving as Hogwarts in the Harry Potter movies. Discover its spectacular grounds, which include Knight's Quest and the Poison Garden.

b. Bamburgh Castle is perched on a rocky outcrop with a sea view. It has a long history and provides breathtaking views from its turrets.

c. Discover the ancient ruins of Warkworth Castle, which are tucked away next to the River

Coquet. The town itself has beautiful streets and a riverbank stroll, making it appealing.

d. The Elizabethan Walls of Berwick-upon-Tweed, which provide sweeping views of the town and the shoreline, maybe walked.

6.2 Galleries and Museums

Explore Northumberland's museums and galleries to learn more about its cultural history and creative expression.

a. The Alnwick Garden has fascinating artworks and exhibits that provide a modern touch to the historic setting in addition to its beautiful grounds.

b. Woodhorn Museum: The Woodhorn Museum has interactive exhibitions, art galleries, and a look into the area's industrial past. Discover Northumberland's mining heritage there.

c. The Granary Gallery: Located in Berwick-upon-Tweed, The Granary Gallery offers a venue for both classic and modern art while showcasing local and international artwork.

6.3 Ancient Churches and other Attractions

Visit Northumberland's ancient churches and monuments to learn more about the region's spiritual and architectural legacy.

a. Hexham Monastery is a magnificent Saxon-era monastery with elaborate woodwork and breathtaking stained-glass windows.

b. The historic and religious importance of Lindisfarne Priory, which is situated on Holy Island, cannot be overstated. It provides a window into Northumberland's history and is accessible at low tide.

c. Dunstanburgh Castle is a well-liked location for photographers and history buffs because of its magnificent castle ruin and the beautiful Northumberland seaside background.

d. Flodden Battlefield: This location serves as a somber reminder of the Battle of Flodden, a pivotal historical event. Interpretive exhibits provide light on the effects of the conflict.

Explore the castles, art galleries, and historical sites of Northumberland to fully immerse yourself in the region's rich history and culture. Every location has a piece of the area's history, enabling you to go back in time and learn more about its past.

7. Dining and Local Cuisine

7.1 Traditional Northumberland Cuisine

Enjoy the traditional foods of Northumberland that are firmly established in the local culture.

a. A circular, dense bread often stuffed with ham, pease pudding, bacon, or sausages is known as a stottie cake. It's a substantial and hearty supper.

b. Using layers of potatoes, onions, and cheese, Pan Haggerty is a warming meal that is pan-fried till brown and crispy.

c. A local favorite, Craster Kippers are smoked herring filets from Craster. You may have them for breakfast or as a tasty snack.

d. Sweet griddle cakes called Singin' Hinnies are baked with flour, butter, sugar, and currants. Frequently, they come with butter and jam.

7.2 Seafood Specialties

Due to its coastal position, Northumberland provides an abundance of fresh seafood that food lovers just must experience.

a. Crab: Try freshly caught crab that has been cooked in a variety of ways, such as crab cakes and sandwiches, to showcase the delicate taste of the sea.

b. Kippers: As was already said, Craster kippers are a standout, providing a deep, smokey flavor that is authentically Northumberland.

c. Fish and chips are a traditional British favorite that is best savored when lounging by the water.

7.3 Taverns and Dining Rooms

By eating in the region's quaint pubs and restaurants, you can learn about Northumberland's culinary scene.

a. The Jolly Fisherman, located in Craster, is a quaint tavern with breathtaking ocean views that serves a variety of seafood meals and regional ales.

b. Dine among the trees in Alnwick's The Treehouse Restaurant, which combines inventive food with ingredients that are obtained locally.

c. The Potted Lobster in Bamburgh specializes in seafood and serves meals made from the newest North Sea harvests.

d. The Bait Box in Amble is a seafood shack that offers recent catches in a laid-back atmosphere, making it the ideal place to eat near the water.

The cuisine of Northumberland reflects its traditional traditions and seaside history. Dining in the area is a sensory experience that tantalizes your taste senses while providing an insight into its cultural legacy, from hearty traditional cuisine to gourmet seafood concoctions.

8. Shopping and Souvenirs

8.1 Local Markets

Discover the thriving local markets in Northumberland where you can buy anything from fresh food to handcrafted items.

a. Alnwick Market: This crowded market sells a range of products, including local vegetables, apparel, and handmade items. It's a terrific location to meet locals since it's held right in the middle of Alnwick.

b. Find a wide variety of locally produced produce, artisanal delicacies, and one-of-a-kind crafts at the Berwick-upon-Tweed Farmers' Market in this lovely town.

c. Amble Sunday Market: This market in Amble, which is held every Sunday, has vendors offering fresh seafood, baked products, crafts, and antiques.

8.2 Artisan Crafts

Buy handcrafted goods from Northumberland to bring a bit of the region's ingenuity and workmanship home.

a. Discover handcrafted ceramics and pottery that are influenced by the history and landscapes of Northumberland.

b. Textiles and woolens: Look for locally produced textiles including high-quality wool blankets, scarves, and apparel.

c. Jewelry and Accessories: Discover one-of-a-kind accessories made by regional artists, often with inspiration from the sea and environment.

8.3 Unique Souvenirs

Northumberland has a wide selection of unique souvenirs that perfectly encapsulate the spirit of the area.

a. Craster Kippers: Smoked kippers are a tasty and well-known local delicacy that is a great way to bring a taste of Northumberland home.

b. Puffin souvenirs from the Farne Islands are a sweet way to remember your trip and honor the area's distinctive biodiversity.

c. Historical Books: Discover the past of Northumberland by reading books on the region's castles, customs, and folklore.

d. Decorate your house with amazing art prints and photographs that depict Northumberland's breathtaking scenery.

Buying gifts in Northumberland is a chance to support regional makers and take home sentimental keepsakes that showcase the area's culture and natural beauty. The markets and stores in Northumberland provide a wide range of options, whether you're looking for handcrafted products, artisanal foods, or one-of-a-kind souvenirs.

9. Festivals and Events

9.1 Year Round Calendar of Events

Northumberland has several events all year round that highlight its culture, history, and natural splendor.

a. Alnwick Food Festival (September): A celebration of regional cuisine and drink with market booths, cooking classes, and tastings.

b. The annual Berwick Film & Media Arts Festival (September/October) features interactive installations and exhibits in addition to experimental and foreign films.

c. August's Berwick Food & Beer Festival offers the chance to sample regional cuisine and breweries while also enjoying live entertainment and beer samples.

9.2 Seasonal Festivals

Discover Northumberland's holiday cheer by attending one of its seasonal events or festivities.

a. The Northumberland Music Festival, which takes place in November, showcases classical music concerts that bring the county's rich history to life.

b. Get into the holiday mood at the Alnwick Christmas Market in December, which offers festive vendors, entertainment, and the chance to see Santa Claus.

c. Christmas shopping may be done in a gorgeous setting at the Berwick-upon-Tweed Christmas Market (December), which has a variety of booths selling crafts, presents, and festive food.

d. Alnwick International Music Festival (July/August): This summer festival honors many musical genres with concerts, seminars, and street entertainment.

Northumberland's year-round calendar is packed with events that let you immerse yourself in the region and its culture, from culinary festivals to cultural festivities. Seasonal festivals provide a chance to take part in the region's festive customs and make enduring memories. Watch out for event dates so you can schedule your trip appropriately and take part in the exciting Northumberland scene.

10. Practical Information

10.1 Emergency Contacts

Make sure you have easy access to the necessary contacts for a worry-free journey.

a In case of police, fire, or medical emergencies, dial 999.

b. Police Non-Emergency: 101

c. VHF Channel 16 or 999 for the coast guard Embassies/Consulates: (If necessary, please include pertinent embassy/consulate details.)

10.2 Currency and Banking

Recognize the accessible payment methods and currencies in Northumberland.

a. The British Pound Sterling (GBP) is the country's official currency.

b. Although credit and debit cards are extensively used in towns and cities, it is still advisable to have some cash on hand, particularly in more remote locations.

c. For easy access to cash, ATMs (cash machines) are often found in cities and villages.

10.3 Essential Travel Tips

Utilize these practical travel tips to make the most of your vacation.

a. Weather: Even in the summer, Northumberland's weather may change quickly, so make sure to carry heavy clothing and be ready for rain.

b. Seasonal Considerations: Verify the hours of operation of attractions since some may change during the year.

c. Parking: If you're driving, be aware that space may be scarce in well-liked tourist destinations. If park-and-ride services are offered, think about utilizing them.

d. Tides: To protect your safety and to explore tide pools and other phenomena while visiting coastal locations, be aware of the tidal timings.

10.4 Essential Packing Checklist

Pack sensibly to ensure a comfortable and pleasurable trip to Northumberland.

a. Pack layers-friendly, multipurpose clothes, including waterproof gear. For exploring, it is essential to have sturdy walking shoes.

b. Electronics: Don't forget to pack power banks, chargers, and adapters for your gadgets.

c. A basic first aid kit and any essential drugs should be carried.

d. Outdoor Gear: Pack the necessary items, such as a daypack, water bottle, and sunscreen, if you want to go cycling or trekking.

e Travel documents: Keep your passport, travel insurance information, and lodging information in a safe, convenient location.

You will enjoy your Northumberland adventure with confidence if you are organized and well-prepared, knowing that you have the essential requirements necessary for a simple and enjoyable trip.

11. Suggested Itineraries

11.1 3-Day Coastal Exploration

- Day 1: Tour the gardens and castle at Alnwick. Take a stroll around the town and then lunch somewhere nearby.

- Day 2: Explore Bamburgh Castle before relaxing on Bamburgh Beach. meal of seafood in the evening.

- Day 3: Depart from Seahouses and take a boat cruise to the Farne Islands. Take a walk around Berwick-upon-Tweed walls to wind down the day.

11.2 4-Day Historical Heritage Tour

- Day 1: Investigate the area around Hexham Abbey. To experience a little of Roman heritage, go to Corbridge nearby.

- Day 2: Explore Holy Island's Lindisfarne Priory. Attend Beadnell Bay for the afternoon.

- Day 3: Tour Warkworth Castle before traveling to Amble for a lunchtime harborside.

- Day 4: Explore Berwick-upon-Tweed by getting out and about, going to the local museums, and taking in the atmosphere.

11.3 2-Day Countryside Escape

- Day 1: Take a tour of the Kielder Water Park and Forest. Enjoy the nighttime sky.

- Day 2: Take a climb through the Cheviot Hills or stroll along the Northumberland Coast Path to take in the breathtaking coastline vistas.

11.4 Smartphone Photography Tips

a. Golden Hours: For breathtaking landscape photographs, capture the warm, soft light during dawn and dusk.

b. Include intriguing items in the foreground of your images to give them depth and perspective.

c. Rule of Thirds: Assume that two vertical and two horizontal lines will divide your image into nine equal parts. For a balanced composition, put important items along these lines or at their intersections.

d. Use leading lines to direct the viewer's attention across the image, such as shorelines, trails, or roadways.

e. Symmetry and Reflections: To produce aesthetically arresting photographs, look for symmetrical settings or water reflections.

f. Use your smartphone's macro mode to experiment and capture the fine details of flowers, insects, and textures.

g. Use portrait mode to take beautiful pictures that are subject-focused and have a blurred backdrop.

h. Editing Tools: Use tools like Lightroom or Snapseed to improve your images. Make your photographs pop by adjusting the exposure, contrast, and colors.

i. Authentic Moments Can Be Captured By Taking Candid Pictures of Locals, Wildlife, and Other Travelers.

j. Try diverse angles, heights, and views to bring creativity and originality to your photographs.

With these pointers, your smartphone may be an effective tool for capturing Northumberland's beauty and making priceless memories.

12. Conclusion

You would take memories of Northumberland's breathtaking scenery, extensive history, and kind people with you when your trip finally ends. Northumberland provides a genuinely memorable holiday with its beautiful coastal towns and delectable regional food.

Northumberland surely made its stamp on your heart, whether you visited its castles, strolled along its beaches, or immersed yourself in its cultural legacy. May your thoughts of this beach getaway inspire and enliven your travels as you return home.

Safe travels, and we hope to see you again in Northumberland soon to make more priceless memories and discover new worlds.

Printed in Great Britain
by Amazon